Fun Fan Facts:
The Unofficial NBA Edition

Indiana Pacers

Everything Young Pacers Fans Should Know

By: Jake Liam

Dedication

For the Pacers fans who survived the Malice at the Palace, the Reggie Miller heart attacks, and still show up every season with full belief.

You are built different. This one's for you.

THE NBA
BY THE NUMBERS

MOST NBA CHAMPIONSHIPS*

CELTICS (18)

LAKERS (17)

WARRIORS (7)

BULLS (6)

SPURS (5)

As of the 2024-25 Season. †One Trophy = 4 Championships.

NBA HISTORY SNAPSHOT

1946 NBA Founded

1954 Shot Clock Introduced

1979 3-Point Line Added

2023 NBA Cup Introduced

BIG NUMBERS

$156 million
Stephen Curry's est. earnings in the 24-25 season

7'7"
Tallest player in NBA history (Gheorghe Mureşan & Manute Bol)

---

30 Teams Competing in the NBA

4 Playoff Rounds

82 Games Per Season

INDIANA PACERS
IN THE NBA

- FOUNDED: 1976 †
- NBA TITLES: 0
- CONFERENCE TITLES: 2*

38 Playoff Appearances

*† Founding dates are complicated & may cause arguments at Thanksgiving. Ask someone born before color TV. All Titles reflect pre-relocation franchise history. * As of 2024-25 Season.*

NBA ALL-TIME MVP LEADERS

KAREEM ABDUL-JABBAR (6) ★ MICHAEL JORDAN (5) ★ BILL RUSSELL (5)

EASTERN CONFERENCE

Atlantic – **Celtics**
Atlantic – **Nets**
Atlantic – **Knicks**
Atlantic – **76ers**
Atlantic – **Raptors**
Central – **Bulls**
Central – **Cavaliers**
Central – **Pistons**
Central – **Pacers**
Central – **Bucks**
Southeast – **Hawks**
Southeast – **Hornets**
Southeast – **Heat**
Southeast – **Magic**
Southeast – **Wizards**

WESTERN CONFERENCE

Pacific – **Lakers**
Pacific – **Clippers**
Pacific – **Warriors**
Pacific – **Suns**
Pacific – **Kings**
Northwest – **Nuggets**
Northwest – **Timberwolves**
Northwest – **Thunder**
Northwest – **Trail Blazers**
Northwest – **Jazz**
Southwest – **Mavericks**
Southwest – **Rockets**
Southwest – **Spurs**
Southwest – **Pelicans**
Southwest – **Grizzlies**

Introduction

Welcome, fans! Whether you're new to cheering for the Indiana Pacers or you've been bleeding the team colors your whole life, this book is packed with fun, exciting facts about your favorite team. Get ready to impress your friends and family with everything you know about the Pacers.

Quick Timeout

This book is packed with stats. Like, A LOT of stats. Every fact was checked, double-checked, and triple-checked. But here's the thing about basketball history: not everyone agrees on everything. Ask someone who watched games before color TV and someone who grew up with instant replay and you'll get two completely different answers. My dad, stepdad, uncle, and grandpa all argued about the same fact. Four people. Four answers. All of them think they're right. So if you spot something that doesn't match what you've heard, congratulations. You might be a bigger fan than the people who helped make this book. And honestly? That's pretty cool.

HOW IT WORKS

THE SEASON
82 Games. One Goal.
Each team plays 82 games.
Win enough to make the
Playoffs.
Every game counts!

PLAYOFFS
30 Teams. 16 Make It.
8 per conference make the playoffs.
Win=Advance | Lose=Go Home
Best record
gets home court!

PLAYOFF ROUNDS
Best of 7. Win 4 or Go Home.
4 rounds of pure pressure.
Every series is do-or-die!

OVERTIME?
5 More Minutes.
Keep playing until
someone pulls ahead.
No ties. Ever.

THE FINALS
One Series. One Champion.
Winner lifts the Trophy.
Legend status unlocked.

How the NBA Works

At first glance, basketball feels simple. Ten players. One ball. Two hoops. Go.

Then the NBA adds the layers.

An 82-game regular season. A draft where bad teams pick first. Playoffs that last two full months. Superstars who can change everything with one trade. Dynasties that rise, fall, and rise again.

And somehow, it all works.

The NBA is built on one big idea: every team gets a chance to reset, reload, and rise again. No relegation. No dropping down to a lower league. Just basketball, every night, from October through June.

It is a league designed for drama, stars, and comebacks. And once you understand the flow, it is impossible to stop watching.

The League Setup

The NBA has 30 teams, spread across the United States and Canada. Those teams are split into two conferences:

- Eastern Conference
- Western Conference

Each conference has three divisions, mostly based on geography. Divisions matter for scheduling, but not as much as they used to.

Every team plays 82 regular season games, usually from October through April. Home games. Road games. Back-to-back nights. Long road trips. The season is a marathon before the sprint even starts.

Win games, and you climb the standings. Lose too many, and the pressure builds fast.

How Games Are Played

An NBA game has four quarters, each lasting 12 minutes. That means 48 minutes of game time, plus timeouts, free throws, and the occasional coach argument that adds another 20 minutes nobody planned for.

Scoring is simple:

- A shot inside the three-point line is worth 2 points
- A shot beyond the arc is worth 3 points
- Free throws are worth 1 point

If the score is tied at the end of regulation, the game goes to overtime, which lasts 5 minutes. Still tied? Another overtime. Keep going until someone wins.

There is a shot clock too. Teams have 24 seconds to take a shot. No standing around. No holding the ball forever. Keep it moving.

The Regular Season Race

The regular season is long for a reason. It tests everything.

Depth. Health. Focus. Patience.

Teams play opponents from both conferences, but they face conference rivals more often. By the end of the season, each conference's top teams have earned their playoff spots the hard way.

The goal is simple: make the playoffs. But there is a twist.

The NBA Cup

In 2023, the NBA added something new to the middle of the season. Something with actual stakes. They called it the In-Season Tournament, now known as the NBA Cup.

It works like this: Every team plays a small group stage during November and December, with special court designs that look like nothing else in basketball. The best teams advance to a knockout round held in Las Vegas.

The winners split a prize pool. Players earn bonus money. And for the first time, a team could lift a trophy before the playoffs even started.

Some fans are still warming up to it. Some players love it. But the moment a team starts treating it seriously and a crowd shows up buzzing in December, it feels like something.

Which, honestly, sounds about right.

The Play-In Tournament

Instead of sending the top eight teams from each conference straight to the playoffs, the NBA added something new. The Play-In Tournament.

Here is how it works:

- Teams ranked 1 through 6 in each conference are safe
- Teams ranked 7 through 10 fight for the final two playoff spots

The 7 and 8 seeds have an advantage. Win once and you are in. Lose and you still get one more shot. The 9 and 10 seeds have to win twice in a row just to earn a first-round matchup.

It turns the end of the season into a sprint. Every game suddenly matters more. Fans love it. Coaches age rapidly.

The NBA Playoffs

Once the playoffs begin, everything tightens.

Sixteen teams enter. Eight from each conference. Every round is a best-of-seven games series. That means the first team to win four games moves on:

- First Round
- Conference Semifinals
- Conference Finals
- NBA Finals

Home-court advantage matters. Crowds get louder. Rotations get shorter. Superstars play heavier minutes. One bad quarter can flip a series. One great performance can define a career.

By the time the NBA Finals arrive in June, only two teams are left. One from the East. One from the West.

Four wins away from a championship. Four wins away from history.

The NBA Draft: Hope Begins Here

Here is where the NBA gets clever. Every summer, new players enter the league through the NBA Draft. Teams take turns selecting college players, international stars, and teenagers straight out of high school.

The teams that finished with the worst records get the best odds to pick early through the Draft Lottery. It is not guaranteed, but it gives struggling franchises a real shot at changing their future with one pick.

That means one bad season does not doom you forever. It might actually change everything. Some franchises are rebuilt by a single draft night moment.

Hope shows up wearing a new jersey.

No Relegation. All Pressure.

Unlike many global sports leagues, NBA teams never drop down to a lower league. They always stay in the NBA.

That does not mean there is no pressure.

Fans remember losing seasons. Owners make changes. Coaches get replaced. Players get traded. Every year is a test of direction, patience, and belief.

Stars, Systems, and Showtime

The NBA is famous for its stars. But stars do not win alone.

Teams need chemistry. Coaches need systems. Role players need to deliver on the biggest stages. One injury. One hot streak. One trade deadline deal. Any of it can flip a season.

That balance between individual brilliance and team basketball is what makes the league special.

Fast breaks. Buzzer-beaters. Game 7s. And moments that get replayed forever. That is the NBA.

Once you get the flow, it is pure electricity.

Indiana Pacers Facts

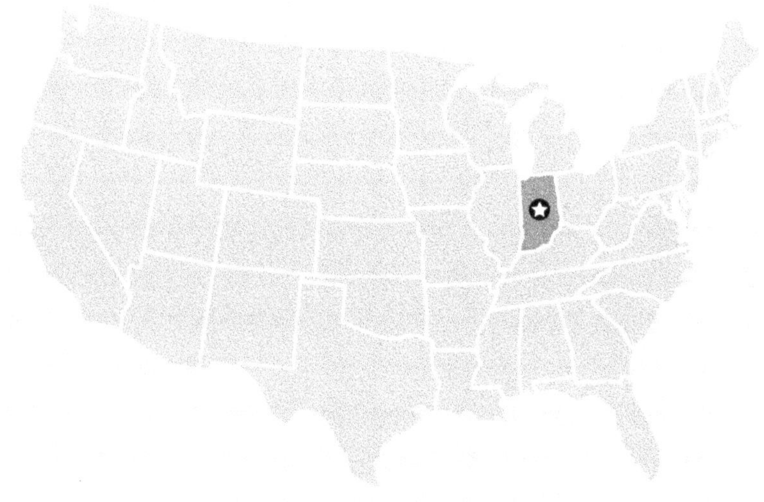

Home City

Indianapolis, Indiana

Home City Metro Area Population

about 2.1 million

Home Arena

Gainbridge Fieldhouse

Max Capacity: 17,923

Famous Local Food

Pork tenderloin sandwich, sugar cream pie, corn on the cob

Conference / Division

Eastern / Central

Chapter 1: Born in the ABA

1. They Built Their Own League Because Nobody Invited Them

In 1967, a group of basketball dreamers looked at the NBA, noticed it only had twelve teams, and decided the solution was not to wait patiently for an invitation. The solution was to start an entirely different league. The American Basketball Association was born that year, loud and chaotic and absolutely convinced it had nothing to prove to anybody. Indiana got one of the eleven founding franchises, and just like that, the Pacers existed.

The ABA wasn't the NBA. The arenas were smaller, the paychecks were thinner, and the league played with a red, white, and blue basketball that looked like it had been designed by someone who really loved the Fourth of July. But the basketball? The basketball was exciting. The ABA pushed a faster, more creative style of play at a time when the NBA was still figuring out whether dunking was too flashy. Indiana was right in the middle of all of it from day one.

The Pacers were not a consolation prize. They were a statement. Indiana already loved basketball more than most states loved anything, and now they had a professional team to prove it. The ABA gave Indianapolis something to believe in, and Indianapolis gave the ABA one of its most loyal fanbases. Not bad for a league that started with a novelty ball and a dream.

2. Three Titles That History Somehow Forgot

The Indiana Pacers are ABA champions. Three times over. They won the title in 1970, 1972, and 1973, and if you did not know that until just now, you are not alone. The ABA has a strange place in basketball history, where incredible things happened and then got filed away under "well, it wasn't the NBA, so does it count?" It counts.

The 1972 and 1973 back-to-back championships were built on a ferocious frontcourt, a suffocating defense, and a team that played with the kind of collective toughness that makes coaches want to cry happy tears. These were not lucky flukes. Indiana was the best team in the ABA for a stretch of years, and they have the trophies sitting in a display case that most basketball fans walk right past without a second look.

Here is what makes it sting just a little: when the ABA and NBA finally merged in 1976, those championships did not come with full historical recognition in the NBA record books. The Pacers entered the NBA as a franchise with a winning history that the new league was in no rush to celebrate. Three titles. Still standing. Just waiting for more people to notice.

3. Why on Earth Are They Called the Pacers?

The name has nothing to do with racing cars, even though Indianapolis is the home of the Indy 500 and that would have been a very easy connection to make. The Pacers were actually named after the harness racing pacers, a type of horse that races while moving both legs on the same side simultaneously in a controlled, efficient gait. Indianapolis had a strong harness racing tradition, and the founders wanted a name that reflected local identity.

There is a second layer to it as well. The pace car at the Indianapolis 500, the vehicle that leads the field before the race begins, was also part of the inspiration. Speed, control, setting the tempo. For a basketball team, there is actually something poetic about being named after the thing that sets the pace. In basketball, controlling tempo is half the game.

So the next time someone asks why a team in a city famous for the greatest car race in the world chose a name connected to horses, you now have the full, slightly complicated, interesting answer. The Pacers are named after a horse and a car and a tradition and a philosophy all at once. Indiana contains multitudes.

4. The League That Invented the Slam Dunk Contest

Every single slam dunk contest you have ever watched, every jaw-dropping, crowd-losing, slow-motion replay moment, traces back to one league. The ABA. In 1976, the American Basketball Association held the very first slam dunk contest in professional basketball history, and Julius Erving, also known as Dr. J, won it with a dunk so spectacular that people who were there still talk about it like they witnessed something supernatural.

The NBA did not invent the dunk contest. The ABA did. The same league the Indiana Pacers helped build, win championships in, and keep alive for nine years before the merger. The NBA eventually borrowed the idea in 1984 and turned it into one of the most watched events in All-Star Weekend, which is great, but the credit belongs somewhere else entirely.

So, the next time you watch a player take off from the free throw line or throw down a windmill and the whole arena explodes, remember where that tradition actually started. A scrappy league with a red, white and blue basketball and a group of teams including your Indiana Pacers decided that basketball should be more fun. Turns out they were right about that.

5. The Merger That Cost Indiana Everything Except Its Dignity

When the ABA and NBA agreed to merge in 1976, it should have been a celebration. Four ABA teams, including the Indiana Pacers, were being welcomed into the biggest basketball league in the world. Instead, it felt like being allowed into a party you were not entirely sure you wanted to attend anymore. The price of admission was steep.

The remaining ABA teams had to pay enormous merger fees to join the NBA, fees that put serious financial strain on franchises that were already not swimming in cash. The Pacers had to sell off players to raise money, dismantling a roster that had been incredibly competitive. The ABA's common draft, which would have allowed remaining teams to share players fairly, was blocked. Indiana entered the NBA older, thinner, and operating on a budget that made it very difficult to compete immediately.

The Pacers did not fold. They did not relocate. They showed up, paid what they owed, rebuilt from scratch, and stayed in Indianapolis. That stubbornness, that refusal to disappear when things got hard, became part of what the Pacers are. Every tough stretch since has been survived because this organization proved in 1976 that it could take a hit, stay standing, and come back swinging. The dignity part was always free.

6. Reggie Miller: The Killer from Compton (1987-2005)

Reggie Miller arrived in Indiana in 1987 as a skinny shooting guard from UCLA who nobody expected to change a franchise. Reggie Miller was not supposed to be this good. He was not supposed to be this annoying. He was especially not supposed to break New York's heart over and over again in front of thousands of people who desperately needed him to miss just once. And yet somehow, across five playoff series against the Knicks in the 1990's, Miller turned Madison Square Garden into his personal stage. New York fans paid good money to watch their team play. They mostly just watched Reggie Miller. For eighteen seasons, Reggie Miller was the most dangerous shooter in basketball and the most theatrical villain any opposing fanbase ever had to deal with. And he enjoyed every single second of it like a man eating a free buffet.

Miller grew up in Compton, California, the younger brother of Cheryl Miller, one of the greatest women's basketball players who ever lived. Reggie spent his childhood getting outplayed by his older sister in the driveway, which did one of two things: either it motivated him completely, or it just meant that nothing on an NBA court ever felt that scary again. He arrived in Indiana as the eleventh pick in the 1987 draft and spent the next two decades becoming the thing every great shooter eventually becomes: someone the other team's fans cannot stop talking about, even when they really want to.

He retired in 2005 as the all-time leader in three-pointers made, a record that held until a guy named Stephen Curry came along and made everyone rethink what was even possible. One gold medal. Over 25,000 points. Eighteen seasons in one city. Never won a championship, which is the one gap on a career so good it almost does not seem fair to mention it.

Reggie Miller launches one of his signature jump shots for the Indiana Pacers. High release. Ice-cold confidence. When Miller got a clean look, defenders could only watch and hope it rimmed out. Photo: Reggie Miller playing for the Indiana Pacers. Photograph by Mshaughn. Licensed under CC BY-SA 3.0. Source: Wikimedia Commons.

7. Rik Smits: The Dunking Dutchman (1988-2000)

Rik Smits is seven feet four inches tall and grew up in the Netherlands, which is a sentence you do not expect to read in a book about Indiana basketball. He was selected second overall in the 1988 draft, arrived in Indianapolis, and spent twelve seasons being one of the most quietly devastating centers in the entire Eastern Conference. He was also, for a man roughly the size of a small building, shockingly difficult to guard, which opposing teams kept learning the hard way every single time they played him.

Smits was not flashy. He did not dance after baskets or wave at the camera or give long speeches about his greatness. He showed up, set screens that felt like walking into a wall, hit mid-range jumpers with creepy consistency, and made opposing centers work incredibly hard for every single point they scored. He was the perfect partner to Reggie Miller's chaos, a big calm presence in the middle who let Reggie handle all the drama while he quietly handled the paint.

His biggest moments came during the 1998 and 2000 playoff runs, where the Dunking Dutchman showed up enormous when Indiana needed him most. He retired in 2000 with over 12,000 career points and a nickname that Indiana fans still say with a huge smile. The Netherlands produced exactly one all-time Pacers legend. They absolutely nailed it on the first try.

8. Mel Daniels: The Big Man the NBA Slept On (1968-1974)

Ask a casual basketball fan to name the greatest centers ever and you will hear the same five names every time. Ask someone who really did their homework and eventually, somewhere in the conversation, Mel Daniels comes up. Daniels played for Indiana from 1968 to 1974 and was, by any honest measure, the most dominant big man the ABA ever produced. He won two league MVP awards, led Indiana to three championships, and made life absolutely miserable for anyone who tried to get comfortable near the basket.

Here is the wild part. Daniels was originally drafted by an NBA team in 1967 and chose the ABA instead. On purpose. At a time when most players would have done anything to be in the NBA, Daniels looked at Indiana and said this is where I am going. He then went out and became the best player in the entire other league, which is a pretty good way to make a point.

The Basketball Hall of Fame finally called in 2012, which was absolutely the right decision and also about forty years later than it should have been. Better late than never, though Mel Daniels probably had some thoughts about the timing that were not suitable for a children's book. Indiana never forgot him. He stayed connected to the franchise for decades, coaching and mentoring and being exactly the kind of legend a city deserves to keep.

9. Paul George: The Homegrown Star (2010-2017)

Paul George was drafted by Indiana in 2010 and immediately looked like a project. Long, athletic, full of potential that had not quite turned into results yet. Three years later he was an All-Star. Two years after that he was finishing second in MVP voting and carrying a Pacers team that had the best record in the entire Eastern Conference. The jump from promising to genuinely great happened so fast that Indiana barely had time to fully appreciate it before things got complicated.

George was the kind of player who made basketball look unfairly easy. He could guard the opponent's best player on one end, then come down and score from anywhere on the other. He became PG-13, a nickname that fit perfectly for reasons that were partly about his jersey number and partly about the fact that his game had just enough edge to make opposing coaches uncomfortable. Indiana loved him, and for a good stretch of years he was exactly the player this fanbase deserved.

Then came the broken leg in 2014, the long road back, the comeback, and eventually the trade to Oklahoma City in 2017 that stung in the way only losing a homegrown star can sting. George went on to win games with another team, which stung a little differently. Indiana got solid pieces back and started rebuilding. Pacers fans still speak about George with real warmth, because what he gave this city during those peak years was genuine, and you do not just forget genuine.

10. Roger Brown: The Man the NBA Banned for No Good Reason (1967-1975)

Roger Brown should have been an NBA player. Everyone who watched him knew it. The NBA knew it too, which makes what happened to him one of the most unfair stories in basketball history. In the early 1960s, Brown was accused of associating with people involved in illegal gambling as a young player. He was never charged with anything. He was never found guilty of anything. The NBA banned him anyway, and the ban lasted long enough to wipe out the best years of his career before they even started.

Brown ended up in Indiana when the ABA launched in 1967, and what came next was one of those stories that makes you glad something worked out while also being furious it had to work out this way. He became one of the most skilled forwards in professional basketball, a creative scorer who could get his shot against anyone and finish with either hand. He was a key part of all three championship teams and one of the most beloved players in Indiana history, which only makes the original ban feel more ridiculous in comparison.

The Basketball Hall of Fame inducted him in 2013, more than twenty years after he passed away in 1997. Brown never received anything close to a real apology for what the NBA did to him. Indiana remembered him and honored him when the rest of basketball had long moved on. That matters. It is also not nearly enough. But out of everywhere he could have landed, he landed here, and Indiana made sure his story did not disappear.

11. Eight Points in Nine Seconds: The Heist Nobody Saw Coming

The New York Knicks were winning. They were up by six points with less than eleven seconds left in Game 1 of the 1995 Eastern Conference Semifinals, and the entire Madison Square Garden crowd was already mentally writing the recap. Game over. Pack it up. See you in Game 2. The only person in the building who had not received this information was Reggie Miller, which turned out to be a fairly significant problem for everybody rooting against him.

What happened next takes longer to explain than it took to actually happen. Miller caught the ball and hit a three-pointer. Then he stole the inbound pass before New York could even breathe, stepped back, and hit another three-pointer while getting fouled on the shot. He calmly made both free throws. Eight points. Nine seconds. One man. An entire arena full of people who went from celebrating to staring at the scoreboard like it had personally insulted them.

Indiana won the game in overtime. The Knicks, to their credit, won the series, which softened the blow slightly for New York fans but did absolutely nothing to remove those nine seconds from basketball history. They are still there. They will always be there. Reggie Miller scored eight points in nine seconds at one of the most famous arenas in sports, and if you close your eyes and really think about it, you can still hear the silence that followed.

12. Reggie Miller vs. Spike Lee: The Greatest Rivalry Nobody Paid a Ticket For

Spike Lee is a famous film director. He is also, by his own enthusiastic admission, the most devoted New York Knicks fan on the planet. He sits courtside at Madison Square Garden in custom Knicks gear, he screams at referees with the energy of a man who has nothing to lose, and for one glorious stretch of playoff basketball in the 1990s, he decided that his greatest enemy was a shooting guard from Indiana named Reggie Miller.

The back-and-forth between Lee and Miller became its own subplot running underneath every Knicks-Pacers playoff series. Miller would score, point at Lee, gesture wildly, and generally behave like a man who had been waiting his entire life for a famous person to argue with courtside. Lee would respond. The crowd would go absolutely berserk. The referees would try to remember they were supposed to be watching basketball. It was extraordinary television and even better live.

The thing that made it so special was that both of them loved it. Miller fed off the energy of an angry crowd the way most people feed off a good breakfast. The more the Garden turned against him, the better he played, which is either a superpower or a personality trait that would be very exhausting to live with. Spike Lee, to his credit, kept showing up every single time. That is either loyalty or stubbornness, and in New York those two things are basically the same thing anyway.

13. The Night Larry Bird Took Indiana to the Finals

In June 2000, the Indiana Pacers played in the NBA Finals for the first time in franchise history. They faced the Los Angeles Lakers, who had Shaquille O'Neal and Kobe Bryant and were about to become one of the greatest dynasties of the modern era. Nobody gave Indiana a chance. Indiana did not care.

The Pacers had beaten Philadelphia, Milwaukee, and then the New York Knicks in six games just to get there. They pushed the Lakers to six games in the Finals, which against that particular Lakers team was like showing up to a sword fight and almost winning. O'Neal was essentially unmovable. Bryant was twenty-one years old and already terrifying. Indiana competed anyway, right to the end.

The man who built that team was Larry Bird, who had become Pacers head coach in 1997 after spending his entire playing career as a Celtic making Indiana miserable. In three seasons he took a rebuilding franchise all the way to the biggest stage in basketball. He won Coach of the Year in his very first season, which should not have surprised anyone and somehow still did. He retired from coaching immediately after the series, having done exactly what he came to do and not one thing more. Very Larry Bird. More on what he did next in Chapter 4.

14. The Malice at the Palace: The Night It All Went Wrong

On November 19, 2004, the Indiana Pacers were playing the Detroit Pistons with 45 seconds left and the game already decided. What happened next became one of the most talked-about brawls in NBA history, ended up on every sports highlight reel for the next twenty years, and resulted in suspensions so long that the Pacers essentially lost the rest of their championship window in a single evening. It is not a funny story. It is, however, one of the most important nights in Pacers history, so here it is.

A hard foul led to a confrontation on the court. A cup thrown from the stands hit a Pacers player. Players went into the stands. Fans came onto the court. The arena became chaos in a way that professional basketball arenas are specifically designed to never become. When the dust settled, nine players were suspended, including Indiana's best player, who missed the rest of that season. The Pacers had been a genuine championship contender. By the time everyone came back, the window had quietly closed.

The NBA changed its rules about fan conduct, arena security, and player behavior after that night in ways that are still in place today. Detroit moved on and won a championship that same season. Indiana spent the next several years rebuilding what had been lost in forty-five seconds in Auburn Hills. Pacers fans watched it happen and did what Indiana fans always do: showed up the next season anyway, which at this point should qualify as a superpower.

15. One Game Away: The 1998 Eastern Conference Finals

The 1998 Chicago Bulls were not a team you were supposed to beat. They had Michael Jordan, who was being Michael Jordan for the sixth time in eight years, and Scottie Pippen, and a supporting cast that had spent the entire decade learning exactly how to win at the worst possible moments. Indiana looked at all of that, made the Eastern Conference Finals anyway, and proceeded to take the Bulls to seven games in a series that should not have been that close and absolutely was.

The Pacers pushed Chicago harder than almost anyone had managed all season. They were physical, they were organized, and they had Reggie Miller, who was constitutionally incapable of accepting that some opponents were just unbeatable. Game 7 went to the Bulls by four points. Indiana was one game away from the NBA Finals and one step away from potentially altering basketball history in ways that nobody has ever fully stopped wondering about.

The Bulls went on to beat Utah in the Finals for their sixth championship, and that dynasty quietly ended that summer. Indiana never got another shot at that specific version of a title run. But for seven games in 1998, the Pacers made the most famous team in basketball actually sweat, which is more than almost anyone else managed, and Indiana fans have been quietly proud of that ever since. One game away is not a championship. It is also not nothing.

Chapter 4: Traditions, Mascots, Random Facts & Fun Stuff

16. Indiana Does Not Just Like Basketball. Indiana Is Basketball.

Most states have a favorite sport. Indiana has a religion, and the church is a basketball court, and the sermon is eighty-two games a season plus playoffs if you have done anything right. No state in America has a deeper, more obsessive, more completely unreasonable love for basketball than Indiana, and Indiana would like you to know that it considers this a completely reasonable way to live.

High school basketball in Indiana is not a school activity. It is a civic event. Towns with populations of four hundred people build gyms that seat three thousand, because you need room for everyone and also their cousins and also the cousins of their cousins. The movie Hoosiers, which tells the story of a tiny Indiana school that wins the state championship, is based on a true story and is treated in Indiana roughly the way other places treat national holidays. People cry every time. Every single time.

The Pacers exist inside this culture, which means the expectations are both enormous and deeply personal. Indiana does not watch basketball casually. Indiana watches basketball the way a very serious chef tastes soup, with complete focus and strong opinions and zero tolerance for anything that is not quite right. Being the professional basketball team in a state that breathes the sport is either a privilege or an enormous amount of pressure, and in Indiana it is somehow both at exactly the same time.

17. Boomer the Lion and the Building That Feels Like Home

The Indiana Pacers mascot is a lion named Boomer, which raises an immediate question from anyone paying attention, because Indiana's team is called the Pacers and not the Lions and there is not a lion anywhere in the team name or logo or history. The explanation is that Boomer was introduced in 1991 and Indiana just decided to go with it, which is honestly a more confident move than trying to explain it.

Boomer is beloved anyway, because mascots do not actually need to make logical sense, they just need to entertain children and confuse adults, and Boomer has been doing both for over thirty years. He wears the blue and gold, he does dunks on a tiny trampoline during timeouts, and he has somehow never once been asked to justify why a team called the Pacers has a lion for a mascot. That is the energy.

Gainbridge Fieldhouse, where the Pacers play their home games, is considered one of the better arenas in the NBA and Indiana fans will tell you this unprompted. It opened in 1999, sits right in downtown Indianapolis, and has an atmosphere during big games that makes opposing teams wish they had scheduled a different road trip. The building holds just under eighteen thousand people, and when those eighteen thousand people are loud, which they frequently are, it is the kind of loud that rattles your teeth in a way you did not sign up for but end up respecting.

18. The Knicks Rivalry: When Basketball Got Extremely Personal

The Indiana Pacers and the New York Knicks met in the playoffs five times between 1993 and 2000, which means that for roughly half of every decade two teams spent most of their springs absolutely hating each other in a very public setting. It was not elegant. It was not graceful. It was, by wide agreement, some of the most brutally entertaining basketball the sport has ever produced, and both fanbases have the emotional scars to prove it.

The rivalry had everything a great sports rivalry needs. It had a clear villain depending on which side you were standing on. It had trash talk so good that people still repeat it today. It had physical play that made modern fans wince and 1990s fans nostalgic. It had Reggie Miller doing something unforgivable to New York about every eighteen months, and it had New York fans responding by making Miller the most booed player to ever set foot in Madison Square Garden, which Miller interpreted as a compliment and used as fuel, which made everything worse for everyone cheering against him.

Patrick Ewing versus Rik Smits in the paint. John Starks trying to contain Reggie Miller, which was like trying to hold water in your hands. Coaches on the sideline looking like they were one bad call away from complete collapse. Indiana won some of those series and lost others, but they were never boring, never safe, and never once felt like a game that did not matter. That is the highest thing you can say about a rivalry. These two teams made each other matter more.

19. Larry Bird: Enemy, Coach, President, Legend

Fact 13 tells you what Bird did on the sideline. Here is what he did after he left it. Bird became the Pacers president of basketball operations, which meant the man who spent thirteen seasons as Indiana's most dangerous enemy became the person responsible for building Indiana's future. The Celtic who dismantled the Pacers every spring was now the executive deciding who wore the blue and gold. Indiana chose to find this funny rather than unsettling, which was the right call.

He helped draft Paul George. He made the personnel decisions that shaped the roster for years. He turned a franchise that had just lost its coach into one with a clear direction and genuine ambition. Not with flash or drama, just with the same quiet competitiveness he brought to everything else he ever did.

Bird never got a championship banner in Indianapolis. But he left fingerprints on everything good that happened there for the better part of two decades, which for a man who once spent his career trying to beat Indiana might actually be the more impressive achievement.

20. Blue, Gold, and the Uniform History Nobody Asked For But Everyone Needs

The Indiana Pacers have worn blue and gold since the day they were founded in 1967, which makes them one of the more consistent franchises in professional basketball when it comes to knowing what colors they are. This sounds like a low bar and in the NBA it really is not, because the history of NBA uniform decisions contains some choices that can only be described as ambitious.

The Pacers went through a period in the 1990s where they shifted toward a darker navy blue and added some pinstripes, which was very much a thing teams did in the 1990s because the decade had opinions about fashion that it shared loudly and without apology. They eventually settled back toward a cleaner royal blue that connected more naturally to the franchise's original identity, and the gold has stayed gold throughout, warm and visible and exactly the color of a team that knows what it is.

The current uniforms are actually sharp, which Pacers fans will tell you while also telling you about every other version of the uniform going back to the ABA days with the kind of detail that suggests they have thought about this more than most people think about most things. Indiana fans care about what the uniform means because the uniform represents something real to them. Blue and gold has meant Indiana basketball for nearly sixty years now. That is not just a color scheme. That is an identity, and in a state where basketball is basically a second language, an identity is everything.

21. Tyrese Haliburton: The Point Guard Who Changed Everything

Tyrese Haliburton arrived in Indiana in 2022 as part of a trade that sent Domantas Sabonis to Sacramento, and Pacers fans spent approximately forty-eight hours being unsure how to feel about it before Haliburton picked up a basketball and made the whole thing very clear. He is a point guard who sees the court like he has a map nobody else was given, a passer who finds angles that should not exist, and a shooter who makes opposing defenses argue with each other about whose fault it was.

He was born on February 29, which means he only has a real birthday every four years, which is either very sad or extremely efficient depending on your perspective. By his second season in Indiana he was an All-Star. By his third he was one of the most clutch players in the entire league, hitting shots in moments so big that Indiana fans had started keeping their phones charged specifically so they could watch the replays immediately afterward. He set a Pacers record with 23 assists in a single game, joining Magic Johnson and John Stockton as the only players ever to record back-to-back games with 20 points and 20 assists.

Haliburton is also close friends with Caitlin Clark of the WNBA's Indiana Fever, which means Indiana now has two of the most exciting young basketball players in the country playing in the same city at the same time. The state that breathes basketball managed to pull that off, and it did not even seem surprised about it, because Indiana has always expected this kind of thing to happen eventually.

22. The Run That Made the Whole Country Watch

The 2025 playoffs were supposed to be a learning experience. A fourth-seeded team building confidence, getting some postseason reps, maybe winning a round before meeting someone too big to get past. That is what was supposed to happen. What actually happened was one of the most jaw-dropping playoff runs in recent NBA history, delivered by a team that had apparently not been told which games they were supposed to lose.

Indiana swept past Milwaukee in the first round, which included Haliburton hitting three separate game-winning shots across the series against a Bucks team that kept being shocked this was happening. Then they eliminated the top-seeded Cleveland Cavaliers in five games, a result that sent the entire Eastern Conference into quiet panic. Then they beat the New York Knicks in six games to reach the NBA Finals for only the second time in franchise history, completing a postseason run so unexpected that basketball fans had to keep checking the scores twice to make sure they were reading them correctly.

They faced the Oklahoma City Thunder in the Finals. Oklahoma City had won 68 games that season, which is one of the best records in NBA history. Indiana pushed them to seven games anyway, because this team had spent the entire postseason refusing to acknowledge that certain opponents were too good to beat. Game 7 brought a heartbreaking end, but what Indiana built during those playoffs was real, earned, and proof that this franchise had arrived at something important.

23. The Core That Carried Indiana to the Finals

Tyrese Haliburton got most of the headlines, which was fair, but the 2025 playoff run was never one player's story. Pascal Siakam, signed to a long-term deal before the season, was a relentless force at forward who could score from anywhere and defend anyone. Myles Turner anchored the middle with shot-blocking that made opposing teams think twice about every single drive they considered. Andrew Nembhard was the quiet glue, the guy doing all the things that do not show up first in a box score but absolutely show up in wins and losses.

Aaron Nesmith and Obi Toppin brought the energy off the bench that turned Gainbridge Fieldhouse into a problem for visiting teams. Coach Rick Carlisle, who had already won an NBA championship with Dallas in 2011, built a system that was fast, connected, and incredibly fun to watch, which for a team that had spent some years being not particularly fun to watch was a meaningful shift. The Pacers played with pace and joy and a collective belief that every single possession mattered, which is easy to say and very hard to actually do for an entire playoff run.

What made this core special was that they actually liked each other, which sounds like a small thing and in professional sports is absolutely not a small thing. Teams that enjoy playing together are different to watch, and Indiana's 2025 group was one of those teams that made basketball look like something worth doing together.

24. What It Actually Means to Be a Pacers Fan

Being a Pacers fan requires a very specific set of personal qualities. You need optimism, but the kind of optimism that has been stress-tested. You need patience, but not the passive kind, the active kind where you keep showing up even when showing up requires something. You need to be the sort of person who, when things go wrong in spectacular and unexpected ways, does not walk away but instead texts three people about it and shows up to the next game with your jersey on.

Indiana fans weathered the Malice at the Palace and still filled the arena the next season. They watched Reggie Miller spend eighteen years doing everything except winning a championship and cheered him like a champion anyway. They sat through rebuilding years and coaching changes and roster overhauls and came out the other side with the same blue and gold belief they walked in with. That kind of loyalty is not common. In a league where fans in bigger markets have more options and more entertainment competing for their attention, Indiana fans chose basketball and kept choosing it regardless of what the standings said.

The 2025 Finals run gave Indiana something it had been waiting a long time for: proof that the belief was not wasted. The city of Indianapolis flooded with blue and gold. Fans who had been watching since the Reggie Miller years stood next to kids who had only ever known Haliburton and all of them were doing the same thing. That is what a great sports team does to a city. It gives everyone the same feeling at the same time, and for Indiana that feeling runs very, very deep.

25. The Future Is Blue and Gold

Every great story has a chapter that has not been written yet, and for the Indiana Pacers that chapter is sitting right there waiting, larger and more promising than it has been in a very long time. The franchise reached the NBA Finals in 2025 with a young core, a brilliant point guard, and a coach who has already won at the highest level. The foundation is not something they are still building. The foundation is built. What comes next is the part Indiana fans are going to want to watch very closely.

Haliburton's road back from injury will be one of the most watched comeback stories in basketball, because what he showed during that 2025 playoff run before he got hurt made it very clear what this team looks like when he is operating at full speed. The supporting cast around him is young enough and talented enough to grow into something even more dangerous than what Indiana put on the floor during those playoffs. The pieces are there. The culture is there. The fanbase is absolutely there and has been there through everything.

Indiana is a basketball state. It has been a basketball state since before anyone reading this book was born, and it will be a basketball state long after everyone reading this book has grandchildren of their own. The Pacers are the professional expression of everything Indiana believes about the sport, and right now, for the first time in a while, that expression has a Finals appearance on its resume and a roster that thinks it can add another one. Blue and gold. Built different. Just getting started.

Bonus Trivia Quiz!

You think you are a true Pacers fan? Try this bonus quiz!

1. What year were the Indiana Pacers founded?

A) 1965
B) 1967
C) 1970
D) 1972

2. Which league did the Pacers play in before joining the NBA?

A) The World Basketball League
B) The Continental Basketball Association
C) The American Basketball Association
D) The National Basketball League

3. How many championships did the Pacers win before joining the NBA?

A) One
B) Two
C) Three
D) Four

4. Where did the name "Pacers" originally come from?

A) The pace car at the Indianapolis 500 and harness racing horses
B) The fast pace of Indianapolis city traffic
C) A famous local horse named Pacer
D) The founder's last name was Pace

5. What made Roger Brown's story one of the most unfair in basketball history?

A) He was banned from the ABA for fighting
B) He was banned from the NBA without ever being charged or convicted of anything
C) He was traded away the season before Indiana won its first championship
D) He retired too early due to injury

6. How many seasons did Reggie Miller play for the Indiana Pacers?

A) Twelve
B) Fifteen
C) Eighteen
D) Twenty

7. What is Rik Smits' famous nickname?

A) The Flying Dutchman

B) The Dunking Dutchman

C) The Dutch Destroyer

D) The Giant from Amsterdam

8. Which team did Paul George get traded to in 2017?

A) Los Angeles Lakers

B) Golden State Warriors

C) Oklahoma City Thunder

D) Houston Rockets

9. How many points did Reggie Miller score in nine seconds against the New York Knicks in 1995?

A) Six

B) Seven

C) Eight

D) Nine

10. What did Larry Bird win in his very first season as Pacers head coach?

A) The NBA Championship

B) Coach of the Year

C) Executive of the Year

D) The Eastern Conference title

11. What happened during the Malice at the Palace in 2004?

A) A referee was knocked out during a game
B) The Pacers walked off the court in protest
C) Players and fans got into a brawl that resulted in massive suspensions
D) The arena lost power during a playoff game

12. How many games did Indiana push the Chicago Bulls to in the 1998 Eastern Conference Finals?

A) Five
B) Six
C) Seven
D) Four

13. What is the name of the Indiana Pacers mascot?

A) Pacer Pete
B) Boomer
C) Blaze
D) Indy

14. What record did Tyrese Haliburton tie with his 23-assist game?

A) The NBA single season assists record
B) The Pacers all-time scoring record
C) The most assists in a game by a Pacer, alongside Jamaal Tinsley
D) The most assists in a playoff game in NBA history

15. How far did the Indiana Pacers go in the 2025 NBA Playoffs?

A) Eastern Conference Semifinals
B) Eastern Conference Finals
C) The NBA Finals
D) They missed the playoffs

Super Fan Secret Challenge

Only a true Pacers fan will know this.

(No Answer Provided)

Tyrese Haliburton was born on a date that only appears on the calendar once every four years. But here is the real question for true Pacers superfans: Haliburton joined a very exclusive club when he recorded back-to-back games with 20 points and 20 assists. Which two all-time legends did he join to become only the third player in NBA history to achieve that feat?

A) Magic Johnson and Isiah Thomas
B) Magic Johnson and John Stockton
C) John Stockton and Jason Kidd
D) Magic Johnson and Gary Payton

1. B) 1967

2. C) The American Basketball Association

3. C) Three

4. A) The pace car at the Indianapolis 500 and harness racing horses

5. B) He was banned from the NBA without ever being charged or convicted of anything

6. C) Eighteen

7. B) The Dunking Dutchman

8. C) Oklahoma City Thunder

9. C) Eight

10. B) Coach of the Year

11. C) Players and fans got into a brawl that resulted in massive suspensions

12. C) Seven

13. B) Boomer

14. C) The most assists in a game by a Pacer, alongside Jamaal Tinsley

15. C) The NBA Finals

NBA PLAYOFF BRACKET

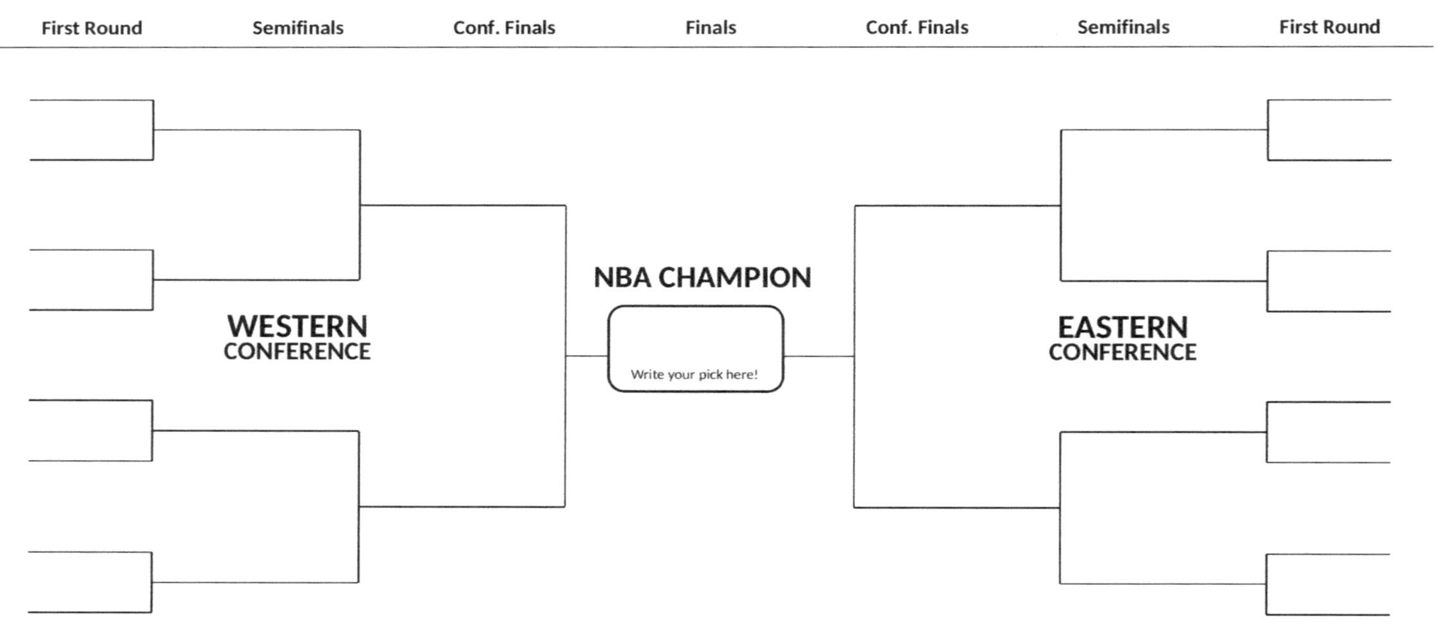

* Fill in your picks and try not to argue with your friends about it!

Part of the Fun Fan Facts: The Unofficial Sports Guide Series

Be the Boss of the Playoffs

You've broken down the matchups. You know which superstar takes over in the fourth quarter. You've seen the bench units that quietly decide series. You've watched the adjustments coaches make when their backs are against the wall.

Now it's time to stop watching and start deciding.

On this page, you are not just a fan. You are the Head Coach drawing up the last play with three seconds left on the clock. You are the GM who built this roster. You are the analyst who saw it all coming.

This is not just filling out a bracket.

This is building your championship run.

Sixteen teams enter the NBA Playoffs. The path is brutal. Best of seven. No shortcuts. No hiding. Every round gets louder, harder, and more personal.

This bracket is your Playoff Control Room.

The Game Plan

1. Survive Round One: Start with the opening round. Which matchup is going seven games? Who has the closer? Who folds under pressure? Make the calls.

2. Feel the Momentum: As you move into the Conference Semifinals and Conference Finals, things change. Role players become heroes. Stars feel the weight. Trust your reads.

3. Own the Finals: Trace your picks all the way to the NBA Finals. When the confetti falls and the trophy is raised, you'll find out who earned it.

House Rules: Circle your boldest upset. That is your official "I knew it" moment.

Choose Your Weapon: Pencil if you want flexibility. Pen if you trust your instincts. Sharpie if you believe in chaos.

Because once the playoffs tip off, there is no rewinding Game 7.

Make your picks. Trust your basketball brain. And let the playoff drama begin.

Fun Facts Wrap-Up

You made it through! You're officially a true superfan! Now it's time to put your knowledge to the test. Share these facts with friends and see who really knows their team best.

Love the series?

Your reviews help other fans discover Fun Fan Facts. If you enjoyed this book, we'd really appreciate you sharing your thoughts and leaving a review.

Want more Fun Fan Facts?

Scan the QR code below to visit our site and explore bonus trivia, challenges, and special extras - including new teams, future series, and collectible fun as they're released.

Collect All the Fun Fan Facts Series!

Check off every book you read. See the full set on Amazon. Search "Fun Fan Facts Jake Liam."

World Cup 2026 Edition

☐ Algeria

☐ Argentina

☐ Australia

☐ Austria

☐ Belgium

☐ Brazil

☐ Canada

☐ Cape Verde

☐ Colombia

☐ Croatia

☐ Curaçao

☐ Ecuador

☐ Egypt

☐ England

☐ France

☐ Germany

☐ Ghana

☐ Haiti

☐ Iran

☐ Ivory Coast

☐ Japan

☐ Jordan

☐ Mexico

☐ Morocco

☐ Netherlands

☐ New Zealand

☐ Norway

☐ Panama

☐ Paraguay

☐ Portugal

☐ Qatar

☐ Saudi Arabia

☐ Scotland

☐ Senegal

☐ South Africa

☐ South Korea

☐ Spain

☐ Switzerland

☐ Tunisia

☐ United States

☐ Uruguay

☐ Uzbekistan

World Cup 2026 Group Edition

☐ Group A

☐ Group B

☐ Group C

☐ Group D

☐ Group E

☐ Group F

☐ Group G

☐ Group H

☐ Group I

☐ Group J

☐ Group K

☐ Group L

English Football Edition

<table>
<tr><td>☐ Arsenal F.C.</td><td>☐ Manchester City</td></tr>
<tr><td>☐ Aston Villa F.C.</td><td>☐ Manchester United</td></tr>
<tr><td>☐ Chelsea F.C.</td><td>☐ Newcastle United F.C.</td></tr>
<tr><td>☐ Everton F.C.</td><td>☐ Tottenham Hotspur</td></tr>
<tr><td>☐ Fulham F.C.</td><td>☐ West Ham United</td></tr>
<tr><td>☐ Liverpool F.C.</td><td>☐ Wrexham A.F.C.</td></tr>
</table>

NBA Edition

<table>
<tr><td>☐ Atlanta Hawks</td><td>☐ Miami Heat</td></tr>
<tr><td>☐ Boston Celtics</td><td>☐ Milwaukee Bucks</td></tr>
<tr><td>☐ Brooklyn Nets</td><td>☐ Minnesota Timberwolves</td></tr>
<tr><td>☐ Charlotte Hornets</td><td>☐ New Orleans Pelicans</td></tr>
<tr><td>☐ Chicago Bulls</td><td>☐ New York Knicks</td></tr>
<tr><td>☐ Cleveland Cavaliers</td><td>☐ Oklahoma City Thunder</td></tr>
<tr><td>☐ Dallas Mavericks</td><td>☐ Orlando Magic</td></tr>
<tr><td>☐ Denver Nuggets</td><td>☐ Philadelphia 76ers</td></tr>
<tr><td>☐ Detroit Pistons</td><td>☐ Phoenix Suns</td></tr>
<tr><td>☐ Golden State Warriors</td><td>☐ Portland Trail Blazers</td></tr>
<tr><td>☐ Houston Rockets</td><td>☐ Sacramento Kings</td></tr>
<tr><td>☐ Indiana Pacers</td><td>☐ San Antonio Spurs</td></tr>
<tr><td>☐ LA Clippers</td><td>☐ Toronto Raptors</td></tr>
<tr><td>☐ Los Angeles Lakers</td><td>☐ Utah Jazz</td></tr>
<tr><td>☐ Memphis Grizzlies</td><td>☐ Washington Wizards</td></tr>
</table>

About the Author

Jake is a 13-year-old sports fan who loves football, American football, and basketball. He plays soccer as a goalie and dreams of one day playing for West Ham United and helping teach kids to love the game. His passion for sports runs in the family - his dad was a professional baseball player, and his stepdad sparked his love for West Ham. Through the Fun Fan Facts series, he shares the fun and excitement of sports with fans everywhere.